YOUR KNOWLEDGE HAS VALUE

Bibliographic information published by the German National Library:

The German National Library lists this publication in the National Bibliography; detailed bibliographic data are available on the Internet at http://dnb.dnb.de .

Imprint:

Copyright © 2012 GRIN Verlag, Open Publishing GmbH
Print and binding: Books on Demand GmbH, Norderstedt Germany
ISBN: 978-3-656-34906-8

This book at GRIN:

http://www.grin.com/en/e-book/207504/digital-branding-a-phenomenon-empowe-red-by-the-internet-and-the-rising

Amelie Lorenzen

Digital Branding - A phenomenon empowered by the Internet and the rising importance of Social Media

GRIN Publishing

GRIN - Your knowledge has value

Since its foundation in 1998, GRIN has specialized in publishing academic texts by students, college teachers and other academics as e-book and printed book. The website www.grin.com is an ideal platform for presenting term papers, final papers, scientific essays, dissertations and specialist books.

Visit us on the internet:

http://www.grin.com/

http://www.facebook.com/grincom

http://www.twitter.com/grin_com

Digital Branding

- a phenomenon empowered by the Internet
and the rising importance of Social Media

"There's never been a better time to be in advertising, and there's never been a worse time." Aaron Reitkopf, North American CEO of digital agency Profero

The Internet has revolutionized the world in many ways. Recently, it seems that both people and organizations have gone all digital. This paper shall give an explanation of Reitkopf's statement on marketing by investigating to what extent the Internet has affected the world of corporate branding and elaborating on advantages and pitfalls of this medium. Arguably, digital branding can be a highly valuable online marketing tool if, and only if, an organization wins the challenge to understand its customers, to successfully establish a positive customer-brand relationship, and to have a comparative advantage over its online competitors.

The structure of this paper his threefold. In the first part, it will derive implications of the Internet and social media on branding in general by elucidating advantages and disadvantages of the digital world. Secondly, the essay will focus on a specific aspect of the so-called I-branding (Simmons,2007), namely co-creation of brands. Lastly, a case study of the sports brand Nike will further clarify the meaning of I-branding and will provide examples for the advantages and disadvantages mentioned in the first part.

The effect of the Internet and Social Media on branding

To start off, the meaning of branding needs clarification. According to Keller (1998), "branding involves attaching a label for identification and meaning for understanding to a product, service, idea, etc. That is, through the manner by which brands and their supporting marketing programs are designed and implemented, brands achieve a certain level of awareness and become linked to a set of associations in consumers' minds." The aim of brands, or in general, their organizations, is to create brand equity which can be defined as "[…]the differential effect that brand knowledge has on consumer response to the marketing of the brand" (Keller, 2008). From brand equity, organizations derive consumer loyalty, larger margins, competitive advantages over competitors, greater price elasticity of demand, brand, category and line extension opportunities, and an increased marketing communication effectiveness (Keller, 2008). Successful branding thus contributes to the creation of brand equity.

Regarding I-branding, organizations have different tools of I-branding at their disposal. In the so-called online brandscape, they possess corporate URLs and pages in social networks, where they present and inform about their products and services as well as where they offer additional features. These features can include product-related and unrelated services such as online shops, store-finder, FAQs, the possibility to obtain information about the organization itself or entertainment features. The latter gain an important role in our topic. Organizations can create digital communities possibly centered on a brand or specific product (Medien Kompakt, 2011) through which users can directly

1

connect with each other and with the brand. Other entertainment features incorporate interaction with the user in the manner of for example games, music, or personalization options. Additionally, users have the possibility to share their interactions with the brand with other users by posting them on their own social network pages, forwarding them via email, or including them in blogs.

The trend of sharing leads to the next argument. Arguably, it has never been easier but also never been more difficult to reach people. As information becomes abundant and simply too much in quantity to possibly absorb, people need sources that reduce the mass of information to a smaller amount specifically relevant for them. On the one hand, online tools such as emails, RSS feeds and social networks support the world of mouth. By enabling users to create profiles and interact with other users, information can be shared and spread, a phenomenon called peer-to-peer (p2p) marketing. Managers and their marketers can "[...] exploit [...] social networks to produce exponential increase in brand awareness, through process similar to the spread of an epidemic (Simmons, 2007)." Sharing information has become easy taking just one click and the spread of content multiplies within seconds. The advantage for branding is that not only the person who initially starts the *epidemic* is a high-potential customer. People connected to this person likely have similar interests and needs and thus become as well part of the target market. Once the process of sharing has started, it develops own dynamics and the organization can be sure that the content spreads. The dynamics base on the fact that people are nowadays "[...]willing to include brand content in their social networking profiles, blogs, and websites, which is an aspect of these generations that businesses should [...] utilize" (Qualman, 2009).

Furthermore, "[...]individuals trust the opinions of their peers more than they trust the opinions presented by traditional advertisements. [...]76 percent of consumers rely on what others say regarding their purchasing decisions, while only 15 percent say they rely on traditional advertising" (Qualman, 2009). This implies, that based on recommendations, people tend to make their consumption decisions instead of searching for content by themselves.

Internet users not only voluntarily help the multiplier effect to come into action but also take over the task of traditional filters such as data agencies and filter the content themselves. On the other hand now, this new kind of filter can arguably be a pitfall for branding. Many users stay within the boundaries of their Internet tools and, beyond those, do not become active and search information on their own. Only information shared by similar interest groups or friends gets through and much content is left behind.

The rationale behind people communicating information is twofold: Information can be interesting, fun or explanatory as well has it can be used for selfish purposes. With the aid of social networks, people do self-marketing and present their identity and personality online. The aim for an individual is to build up a digital self-image that presents oneself in a highly positive way. Marketers exploit this self-image-building by adopting "[...] a more social perspective [...]" (Mühlbacher et al., 2006) and by conceiving"[...] brands as meanings shared by a group of people who use them as symbols in social interaction" (ibid). Salomon (1983) argues that brands provide an important role in identity creation, and customers often decide whether to accept or reject brands on the basis of its symbolic value. The aim is to market a brand or product in a way that the product- or brand image and the self-image are congruent (ibid). If this is the case, people are likely to use a certain brand or product for the purpose of self-image building.

Hence, the challenge for organizations is to build unique, entertaining, and valuable digital marketing programs considered worthy to share. Branding via the Internet then becomes a mutually valuable process both for the brand and for the customer (Simmons, 2007). On the one side, the brand profits because relevant content is shared among a mass of people without having to spread it oneself. On the other side, the Internet user profits since one can present oneself in a certain light using the brand image as contributor to the self-image.

Nevertheless, I-branding, in order to reach consumers' minds, needs to fulfill certain criteria. Simmons (2007) lists four points that need to be considered for traditional but even more for digital branding. He (2007) suggests that successful branding involves more than just the core product or service. Brands have to understand their customers, have to communicate to and position their marketing for the relevant audience, and have to ensure ongoing interactions with target customers. Thereby, the aim is to achieve lasting competitive advantages in the form of brands (ibid). The order of these three steps is essential since the definition of the target market and the understanding of consumer needs has to come first. "New technologies and emerging market trends have converged to shift the balance of power from companies towards customers" (ibid). As customers have become more powerful in the sense that they have powerful tools at hand to either support or undermine content, branding is all about having a strong market orientation and putting consumer needs in focus.

The second step relates to the question how brands are communicated to customers. In his paper, Simmons (2007) includes a study by McKinsey & Company which says that as customers can choose between a wide variety of brands and products and "as functional benefits (e.g. functional quality) become commodities that can be easily replicated, process and relationship benefits increasingly drive purchase decisions and word of mouth." Thus, it is crucial to clearly position a brand in the consumers' minds. Branding means creating brand awareness which can be achieved by increasing the familiarity of the brand through repeated exposure, brand elements, or strong links between brand and category (Keller, 2008). I-branding forces marketers to go "beyond generating awareness [...] to a greater focus on developing trust and relationships [...]" (Simmons,2007). For digital branding, this new way of communication implies the following: Brands have to deliver both content and additional features. Qualman (2009) explains that "companies that find success within social media tend to function more like entertainment companies than traditional advertisers". One challenge is to make virtual branding actually not appear like advertising but more like a conversational and fun marketing. Since most people use social media networks in their free time, marketing should not be perceived as marketing but brands should be "[...] determined more so by the context of delivery than the content delivered" (Kenny & Marshall, 2000). This means that marketers should disguise content in form of a fun or value-adding context of delivery.

The third step mentioned by Simmons (2007) addresses relationship building. Online branding helps consumers build emotional relationships with brands through "[...] targeting customers with unique messages, unique functionality, content and personalization techniques" (Ibeh et al., 2005). Simmons (2007) argues that "[...] as interaction increases, relationships become stronger and more sustainable. Griffith et al. (2001) continue saying that "[...] the utilization of multimedia tools can help to stimulate higher levels of users' brand involvement [...]". Building an emotional bond and thus consumer loyalty entails that Internet users need to become active themselves. This can be achieved through various ways such as co-creation. Moreover, the enhanced proximity between brands and consumers enables organizations to build up a brand personality online and even provide the brand with human traits. Human elements, again, boost a brand's likeability (Keller, 2008).

The brand-consumer proximity also becomes clear when looking at the fact that newsletters, RSS-feeds, emails, blogs, or online communities allow brands a constant presence in the consumer world. Mostly, the consumer even voluntarily permits the brand to enter his or her private life by signing up for receiving information, sharing content, or engaging oneself in the online brandscape. Thus, digital branding implies a "[...] systematic process of understanding, attracting, engaging, retaining and learning about target customers" (Simmons, 2007).

In addition to a constant presence, branding efforts need to show a clear consistency. Because the Internet offers organizations such a variety of tools, they have to serve many of them with the aim of reaching the largest possible customer mass in order to generate strong, favorable and unique associations, Qualman (2009) explains that "[...] organizations should work to craft one simple and salient message that will convey throughout all of their marketing tactics [...] via social media marketing". If inconsistent, I-branding engenders confusion and dilutes brand equity.

As a matter of fact, the constant presence of brands implies advantages and disadvantages. In its ruthlessness and transparency, the Internet exceeds any other medium of branding. What once enters the Internet, spreads within seconds on a global scale, will never leave it and is openly accessible to anyone. Besides, no medium listens to peoples' needs as the Internet does. "[...] Social media [for example] allow dissatisfied customers to post their complaints right away, in the height of their frustration (Qualman, 2009)." The malfunction of websites disappoints consumers and entails complaints posted on the Internet. Negatively interpreted, this transparency can destroy all branding efforts and, as a consequence, severely dilute brand equity since unfortunate brand associations are elucidated. Positively interpreted, this transparency "[...] gives companies a unique opportunity to gain authentic insight into the problems that customers are facing when using their product or service" (ibid). Consumers thus serve as a source of knowledge and improvement which helps organizations to better grasp consumer needs. Because I-branding means a constant process of learning, organizations can customize products and supporting marketing programs exactly to consumer needs in the long run. Hence, they achieve strong, favorable, and unique brands associations which successfully add to brand equity and mean a source of growth for the whole company (Keller, 2008). Compared to traditional marketing efforts, "interactive conversations are much more effective than one-way projections when it comes to engaging the voting audience" (ibid).

This interaction however requires a certain degree of consumer responsibility. Because the Internet and its tools are so complex and sometimes even difficult to understand, the danger exists, that a too high complexity of I-branding efforts leads to uncertainty among customers (Piller, Berger, Möslein & Reichwald, 2003). High uncertainty again elicits negative brand associations and consumers will probably switch to brands that are easier comprehensible.

Competition in general has sharpened with the birth of I-branding. Because it is so cheap to publish in the Internet, even small organizations with low budgets have the possibility to brand their products online. Switching to a competitor takes consumers just one click. In general, marketers need to be aware of the extremely high pace that the Internet and technological advances entail. If lucky, successful branding of a product or service leads to an Internet hype and everyone will talk about it. But, as fast as a hype is created, as fast it can disappear. Generally, the "marketing life cycle" for a product or service on the Internet is much shorter than in traditional media meaning that I-branding has to be achieved either very quickly or with the aid of long-term marketing programs which retain consumers over larger spans of time and can last even hypes. The success of online branding as opposed to traditional one can then be explained by the constant presence in the target market instead of launching temporary or seasonal branding efforts. The defy thus is to build a sustainable competitive advantage which implies the urge to stay innovative and to always follow the latest technological advances of the Internet.

Co-creation

Co-creation is an example of a branding tool helping brands to achieve a comparative advantage over competitors. This part of the paper will focus on customer-direct co-creation empowered by the Internet. Co-creation by definition provides an outlet for brands to include customers in the product and marketing planning process and has become a driving force in social media and marketing technique (Social Media Forum, 2011). Hereby, the link to I-branding is the following: branding in general is about labeling and providing a meaning for products. This can be obtained through a branding strategy that clearly differentiates the product from other competitive ones. The Internet helps organizations to obtain a powerful source of differentiation, of which co-creation is a very good example. They can propose consumer collaboration on their online domains which then necessarily brings about consumer participation and an increase in the emotional value of the co-designed product (Berger & Piller, 2003).

On the marketer's side, co-creation changes the role of traditional marketers, a phenomenon which Piller, Berger, Möslein & Reichwald (2003) call a "[...] transition from product marketer to solution provider". As opposed to just buying the product, Internet users have the chance to directly participate in the process of designing the product and to share their co-design afterwards with other users worldwide via social networks. Sharing one's design with others is argued to be a natural extension of co-creation reasoning the terminus "social co-creation" (Sloan, 2010). The motive why people share their private life with others and thereby helping the brand to enhance its reputation originates in the idea of self-marketing elaborated in the first section of the paper. Consequently, social co-creation sets a mutually valuable process in action. On the one hand, people add up to their own "self-equity", on the other hand organizations improve their operational performance and their competitive position (Berger & Piller, 2003).

A further advantage of social co-creation is the possibility to cut expenses. Since co-creation connects consumer and brand directly, marketers can reduce market research efforts having a digital constant learning factory with global real-time data at hand. Engaging customers in the product and marketing planning process also means an infinite source of creativity, open innovation and a potential innovation leadership (ibid). Innovation as brand-building tool provides brands with a competitive advantage and establishes a certain reputation in the target market (ibid). Not only for the co-created goods the learning effects are valuable but also for other ones, which can result in synergies between co-created and traditional products (ibid). Ultimately, synergies can entail economies of scope for the whole organization. More potential savings include a decreased fashion-risk since the product is tailored to consumer needs and subsequently the avoidance of overstock. Also, expenses can be cut due to the direct selling process which avoids the involvement of intermediaries such as retailers.

On the contrary, co-creation and the learning effect also incorporate pitfalls. As only a relatively small fraction of consumers participate in the co-creation process, the resulting product does not necessarily mirror the needs of the broad mass of consumers. Moreover, an organization has to closely analyze whether co-creation possibly engenders distribution channel conflicts with traditional retail stores and cannibalization conflicts with un-customized products. (Piller, Berger, Möslein & Reichwald, 2003). Also, co-creation can even increase expenses. Re-orders are expensive for the brand since customized products cannot be resold to other customers (ibid). The process of co-creation forces organizations to have adequate manufacturing system, which may be more expensive than regular ones.

Nike

Now, a case study on Nike shall illuminate chances and pitfalls of the Internet and social co-creation listed above. Nike owns the image of being a young, trendy, innovative and engaged brand. It also owns the reputation of being one of the market leaders concerning branding and social co-creation (Swallow, 2011). Applying Keller's (1998) definition of branding to Nike, one can examine the following: Nike uses different channels of marketing, including the traditional one (e.g. advertisement in magazines, sponsors of events, etc.) and the digital one. The digital channel again consists of different marketing efforts. Apart from its URL which includes an online shop, Nike has created an entertaining marketing program (Swallow, 2010). Marketers have initiated blogs, for instance the Nike Basketball Blog informing about any latest Basketball news or new products. With widgets such as Nike+, which is Nike's own social network with around ten million users (ibid), runners can participate in challenges, form teams, recommend running routes, etc. by synchronizing their iPods with their computer and transferring their running information on it. Lastly, Nike participates actively in other famous social networks such as Facebook, YouTube, QQ (China), or Mxit (South Africa) (ibid).

With the mass-customization initiative NikeiD, Nike has created a powerful marketing program. On its corporate website, for an extra charge of around 30 percent, users have the possibility to personalize their clothes and shoes they want to order, then create an online poster of their design and subsequently upload it to their personal Facebook page. By enabling users to shop, connect and use Nike-content for self-marketing purposes in social networks, Nike has improved its operational performance as well as its competitive position (Piller, Berger, Möslein & Reichwald, 2003). According to a research study, 81 percent of consumers are willing to pay more for customized products, 54 percent of custom product buyers consider themselves leaders, which means that they are most likely to tell others about products that interest them (Sloan, 2010). In the fiscal year 2010, Nike increased its web sales by 25 percent to $260 million (ibid). "To Nike, customization and social media are strategic revenue generators" (ibid). Moreover, with NikeiD, the company has achieved to renew the popularity of a normally relatively simple, daily-life product, namely a shoe (Medien Kompakt, 2011).

The company's I-branding efforts are consistent with the overall brand image and complementary to other efforts (Swallow, 2011). Consequently, Nike achieves a high level of brand awareness and creates brand knowledge which results in customers not only owning but also sharing positive associations. Only once, negative news have made the round when the Nike+ site malfunctioned. Nike immediately repaired the site and, reversing unfortunate associations into positive ones, announced to launch a completely new Nike+ site in the spring of 2012 (ibid).

Consequently, the company is an example of successful I-branding because it has attained to impact brand knowledge in a way that the brand can be thought of as labeling products and providing meaning (Keller,1998). In total, Nike as a strong brand, comes to be seen by consumers as highly familiar and characterized by strong, favorable, and unique associations (ibid).

Conclusion

In conclusion, the Internet with its variety of options has taken branding to the next level. Advantages of that include an enhanced proximity to consumers, empowering organizations to have a stronger market orientation, reduced costs with marketing programs being cheaper than traditional ones, and less expenses and efforts on market research but instead global real-time data derived from user profiles and their online activities. Moreover, voluntary p2p-marketing on the Internet complements pure market penetration strategies carried out by organizations. Customers partially take over the role of managers and marketers and set the multiplier effect in action. The Internet empowers brands to attach customers emotionally to them increasing their loyalty, to be always present in their target market, and, owning digitally comparative advantages, gives opportunities for innovation and global growth for the whole organization. Disadvantages are the risk of drowning in the mass of competitors and information, and the risk of diluting brand equity. The chances for I-branding evidently surpass the pitfalls but organizations have to be aware of both and have to develop consistent, entertaining and innovative marketing programs ensuring a constant presence in the online world.

Sources

Berger C. & Piller, F. (2003). Customers as Co-Designers. *IEE Manufacturing Engineer*, 42-45. Retrieved from http://www.mass-customization.de/download/iee03.pdf.

Engaging Social Media for Customer Insight, Co-Creation and Crowd-Sourcing at Social Media World Forum 2011 (2011, February 2). Social Media Forum. Retrieved from http://www.socialmedia-forum.com/blog/2011/02/asia/engaging-social-media-for-customer-insight-co-creation-and-crowd-sourcing-at-social-media-world-forum-europe-2011/

Gouillart, F. (2010, September 30). Co-Creating Campaigns and the Social Contract. Retrieved from http://powerofcocreation.com/authors-blog/co-creating-campaigns-and-social-contract.

Griffith, D.A., Krampf, R.F. & Palmer, J.W. (2001): The role of interface in electronic commerce: consumer involvement with print versus online catalogs. *International Journal of Electronic Commerce*, 5 (4), 135-53.

Ibeh, K.I.N., Luo, Y. & Dinnie, K. (2005): E-branding strategies of internet companies: some preliminary insights from the UK. *Journal of Brand Management*, 12 (5), 355.

Keller, K.L. (1998). Branding Perspectives on Social Marketing. Advances in Consumer Research, 25, 299-302. Retrieved from http://www.acrwebsite.org/volumes/ display.asp?id=7887

Keller, K.L. (2008). *Strategic Brand Management: Building, Measuring and managing Brand Equity*. Upper Saddle River, NJ: Prentice Hall.

Kenny, D. & Marshall, J.F. (2000): Contextual marketing: The real business of the Internet. *Harvard Business Review*, 119-125. Retrieved from http://informationmarketing.net /BrandingAdvertisingMarketing/Quotes /Others/ContextualMarketing.pdf

Medien Kompakt (2011, December). Social Media Best Practice: Nike & Dell. Retrieved from http://www.medienkompakt.de/index.php/social-media-best-practice-nike-dell/.

Mühlbacher, H. et al. (2006). Brands as Social Complex Phenomena. University of Innsbruck   Press. Retrieved from http://clemens.pirker.free.fr/publications/brand_social_phenomenon.pdf

Piller, F., Berger, C., Möslein, K. & Reichwald, R. (2003). Co-Designing the Customer Interface:Learning from Exploratory Research.   Technische Universität München. Retrieved from   http://www.aib.wiso.tu-muenchen.de/neu/eng/content/publikationen /arbeitsberichte_pdf/TUM-   AIB%20WP%20037%20Berger%20Piller%20et%20al %20Co-Designing.pdf

Prahalad, C.K. & Ramaswamy, V. (2004). *The Future of Competition: Co-Creating Unique Values with Customers.* Harvard Business School Press. Retrieved from http://www.sce.carleton.ca/faculty/tanev/TTMG_5005_P/Session_5_Feb_6_2008/Co-creating%20unique%20value%20with%20customers.pdf.

Qualman, E. (2009). *Socialnomics. How Social Media Transforms the Way We Live and Do Business.* Hoboken, NJ: John Wiley & Sons, Inc. Retrieved from http://www.ebscohost.com/uploads/corpLearn/pdf/bbs_socialnomics.pdf.

Simmons, G.J. (2007). I-Branding: Developing the Internet as Branding Tool. Marketing Intelligence & Planning, 25 (6), 544-562.

Sloan, D. (2010, July 19). 5 Signs that Co-Creation is a Trend to Watch. *Venture Beat.*   Retrieved from http://venturebeat.com/2010/07/19/5-signs-that-customer-co-creation-is-a-trend-to-watch/.

Solomon, M.R. (1983). The Role of Products as Social Stimuli: A Symbolic Interactionism perspective. Journal of Consumer Research, 10 (3), 319-329.

Stuart, H. & Jones, C.D. (2004). Corporate Branding in Marketspace. *Corporate Reputation Review*, 7 (1), 84-93. Retrieved from http://eprints.utas.edu.au/821/

Swallow, E. (2011, September 22). How Nike Outruns the Social Media Competition.   *Mashable Social Media.* Retrieved from http://mashable.com/2011/09/22/nike-social-media/.

YOUR KNOWLEDGE HAS VALUE